In My Classroom

By Pamela Chanko

ISBN: 978-1-338-88851-5

Editor: Liza Charlesworth
Art Director: Tannaz Fassihi; Designer: Tanya Chernyak
Photos ©: cover: Karen Roach/Shutterstock.com; 2: nico_blue/Getty Images;
3: ideabug/Getty Images; 4: Kevin Giszewski/Dreamstime; 5: Llewellyn/Alamy Stock Photo;
6: photonic 1/Alamy Stock Photo; 7: m.schuppich/Alamy Stock Photo; 8: FatCamera/Getty Images.

1 2 3 4 5 6 7 8 9 10   68   31 30 29 28 27 26 25 24 23
Printed in Jiaxing, China. First printing, January 2023.

SCHOLASTIC INC.

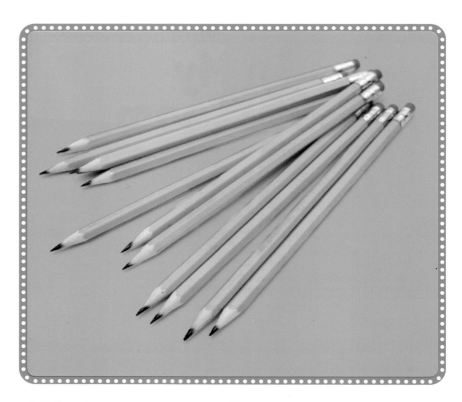

We have pencils.

We have paper.

We have crayons.

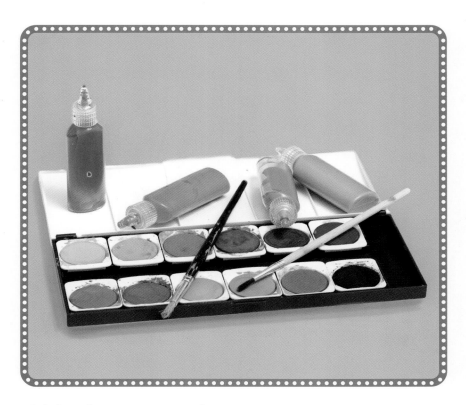

We have paints.

We have books.

We have blocks.

We have kids!